Being a Scientist

Young learners need to know that scientists are not just workers wearing white jackets in laboratories. We do science when we

- cook breakfast
- mix paints to make new colors
- plant seeds in the garden
- watch a squirrel in a tree
- mark how tall we are on a growth chart
- look outside to see what the weather is like

The scientists in the science laboratories and those in the kindergarten or first-grade classroom use important science processes to do their work. This book helps students to recognize and experience those processes.

The activities in this book relate to National Science Education Standards (Science as Inquiry). When you follow the step-by-step lessons, your students will be doing science. They will

- observe
- predict
- compare
- order
- categorize

- ask meaningful questions
- conduct investigations
- record information
- communicate investigations and explanations
- use tools and equipment

What makes this book easy for you?

- The step-by-step activities are easy to understand and include illustrations where it's important.
- The resources you need are at your fingertips—record sheets; logbook sheets; and other reproducibles such as minibooks, task cards, and picture cards.
- Each science concept is presented in a self-contained section. You can decide to do the entire book or pick only those sections that enhance your own curriculum.

minibooks

task cards

logbooks

picture cards

Using Logbooks as Learning Tools

ScienceWorks for Kids emphasizes the use of logbooks to help students summarize and solidify learning.

Logbooks are valuable learning tools for several reasons:

- Logbooks give students an opportunity to put what they are learning into their own words.
- Putting ideas into words is an important step in internalizing new information. Whether spoken or written, this experience allows students to synthesize their thinking.
- Explaining and describing experiences helps students make connections between several concepts and ideas.
- Logbook entries allow the teacher to catch misunderstandings right away and then reteach.
- Logbooks are a useful reference for students and a record of what has been learned.

Two Types of Logbooks

This picture stands for class logbook

As discussions and investigations in this book are completed, the teacher will record student understandings in a class logbook. Even though your students may not be reading, the responses can be read to them as a means of confirming and reviewing learning.

Record student responses on large sheets of chart paper. Pictures drawn by students can be added to illustrate what has been recorded. Use metal rings to hold the pages together.

The class logbook is a working document. You will return to it often to review what has been learned.

This picture stands for student logbook

Students process their understanding of investigations by writing or drawing their own responses in individual student logbooks. Following the investigations are record and activity sheets that can be added to each student's logbook.

At the conclusion of the unit, reproduce a copy of the logbook cover on page 3 for each student. Students organize their pages and staple them with the cover.

page 3

I
Am
a
Scientist

My Logbook

Name:

Teacher Preparation

Before beginning this unit, prepare the following:

- Collect these special tools to use in the experiments in this book:

magnets	various types of thermometers
hand lenses	various types of scales
metal mirrors	flashlight

- You will need goldfish for the observation on page 6.

- Make a class set of "clipboards" for students to use when making observations outside the classroom.

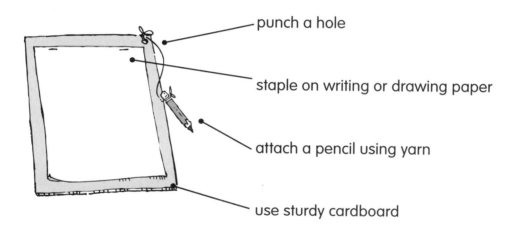

punch a hole

staple on writing or drawing paper

attach a pencil using yarn

use sturdy cardboard

A Science Library

Gather an assortment of science books. (See the inside back cover for a bibliography of books used in *Learning to Be a Scientist*.)

Note: *Use the most up-to-date materials you can find, as new discoveries frequently occur in science.*

Scientists make observations.

What Do Scientists Do?

Ask, "Who can tell me what a scientist is? What does a scientist do?" Answers will depend on the prior knowledge of your students. Return to these questions frequently as students learn more about the actions of scientists.

Making an Observation

• You will need bubble mixture and a wand for this activity. Explain that scientists learn about things by watching carefully to see what happens. Using the bubble mixture, blow a large bubble. Ask students to describe what they see. Ask, "What is inside the bubble? How do you know?" *(Air is in the bubble. We saw you blow air into it.)* Explain to students that they are observing what happens. Say, "Now you are going to be scientists. You are going to observe something carefully."

• In the following three activities, students will be making observations.

Where Did the Water Go?

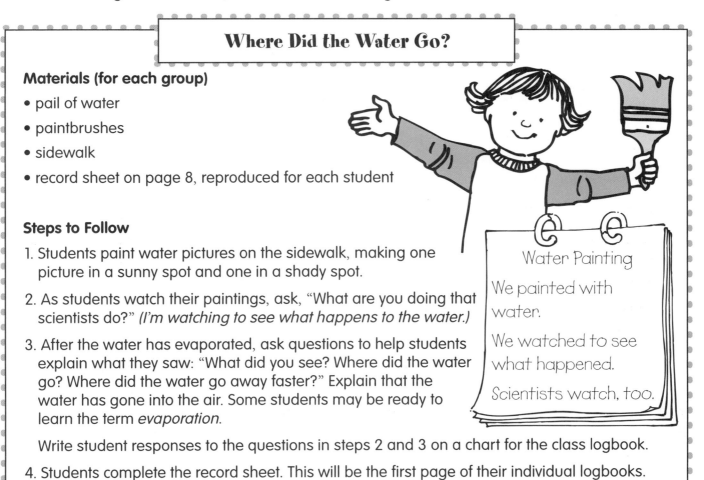

Materials (for each group)

• pail of water
• paintbrushes
• sidewalk
• record sheet on page 8, reproduced for each student

Steps to Follow

1. Students paint water pictures on the sidewalk, making one picture in a sunny spot and one in a shady spot.

2. As students watch their paintings, ask, "What are you doing that scientists do?" *(I'm watching to see what happens to the water.)*

3. After the water has evaporated, ask questions to help students explain what they saw: "What did you see? Where did the water go? Where did the water go away faster?" Explain that the water has gone into the air. Some students may be ready to learn the term *evaporation*.

   Write student responses to the questions in steps 2 and 3 on a chart for the class logbook.

4. Students complete the record sheet. This will be the first page of their individual logbooks.

Water Painting

We painted with water.

We watched to see what happened.

Scientists watch, too.

5   Learning to Be a Scientist • EMC 872

Watch the Goldfish

Show students a goldfish in a bowl. Say, "Scientists watch animals carefully to learn about what they are like and what they do. You are going to watch a goldfish carefully to see what you can learn."

Materials (for each group)

- goldfish in a bowl
- record sheet on page 9, reproduced for each student

Steps to Follow

1. Have each group observe their goldfish for several minutes.

2. Ask students to explain how they have acted like scientists. *(We've been watching carefully to learn about the goldfish.)*

3. Have students share what they have learned. Record their observations on a chart entitled "Learning About Goldfish."

4. Pass out record sheets. Have students observe their goldfish again as they complete their record sheets.

5. Read and discuss *Your First Goldfish* by Mariana Gilbert or *All About Your Goldfish* by B. Bradley Viner. Compare what students learned from their observations with the information in the book. Make additions or corrections to the goldfish chart.

page 9

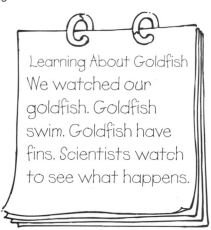

Learning About Goldfish
We watched our goldfish. Goldfish swim. Goldfish have fins. Scientists watch to see what happens.

In My Square

In Our Squares

Scientists watch.
We watch, too.
We watched to see
what was in our
squares.

1. Divide the class into small groups. Mark off an area about one square foot (30.5 cm) for each group somewhere on the school grounds where there will be both plants and small animals (worms, ants, etc.) to observe. Give each student a clipboard holding a sheet of drawing paper and a pencil (see page 4).

2. Students observe their squares for a set period of time. They are to draw what they see in their squares.

3. Back in class, ask students to explain how they acted like scientists. *(We watched to see what was in our square.)* Then ask them to describe what they saw in their square.

   Record their answers from steps 2 and 3 on a chart entitled "In Our Squares."

4. Using page 10, students record in words or pictures what they did and what they saw. Place completed record sheets in students' logbooks.

5. Read and discuss *Backyard—One Small Square* by Donald M. Silver. Ask students to share what they observed in the book's illustrations.

page 10

Name

In My Square

I watched to find out what was in my square.
Draw what you see in your square.

Include these pages in each student's logbook.

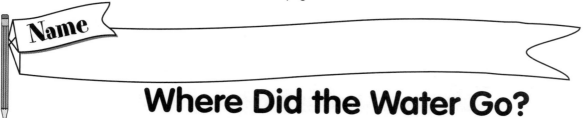

Name

Where Did the Water Go?

I watched to see what happened.

Circle the answer.

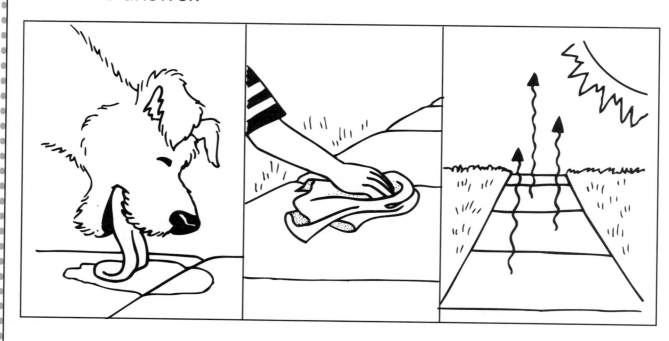

Where did the water go away faster?

Name

Goldfish

I watched to find out about goldfish.

This is what the goldfish looks like.

This is how the goldfish moves.

 Learning to Be a Scientist • EMC 872

Name

In My Square

I watched to find out what was in my square.
Draw what you see in your square.

Sorting and Naming Categories

pages 15–19

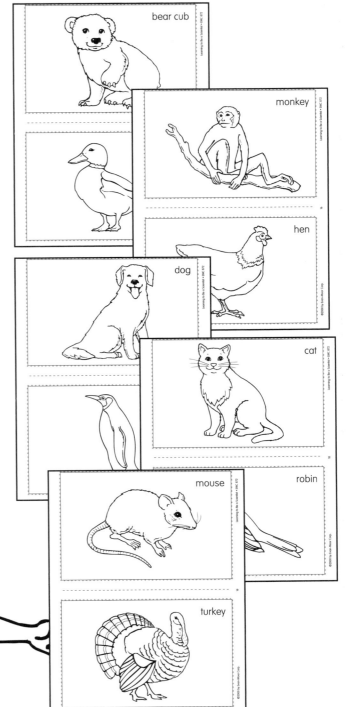

- Reproduce the cards on pages 15–19. Show the pictures of the bear cub and the duck. Ask students to name the pictures. Have two students each hold a picture. Say, "I'm going to show some more pictures. Your job is to decide whether each picture goes with the bear cub or the duck."

When the task is completed, ask students to tell why the animals in each set go together. *(These animals have feathers. These animals have fur.)*

Explain that they have just done something a scientist does—they have put things that are alike into groups called *categories* and given each category a name.

Say, "Now you are going to be scientists. You are going to put more things into categories. Then you will name some of the categories you make."

- In the following three activities, students will be forming and naming categories.

I can be a scientist, too!

Natural or Manmade?

Materials

- an assortment of familiar things—apple, walnut in shell, stick, flower, leaf, pencil, paper clip, tennis ball, stuffed animal, box of crayons, etc.

- record sheet on page 20, reproduced for each student

page 20

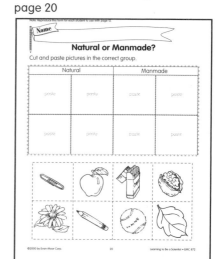

Steps to Follow

1. Show each object you have collected. Ask students to look at each item and determine where it comes from. Use guided questioning to help students sort the items into groups. Record their responses on the chalkboard.

2. When all items have been recorded, use questioning to help students designate two groups that represent "natural" and "manmade." For example, say,

   "Someone said that the flower and the leaf are growing things. Is there anything else on our list that can grow? Did people make these things?" Move all the items named together. Ask, "What would be a good name for this category?" *(Things that grow. Things we find outdoors. Things made by nature.)*

   Have students look at the remaining items. Ask, "Were these things made by nature? Did people make them? What can we name this group?" *(Things we get in stores. Things people make.)*

   Using students' words, create a chart for the class logbook, listing the items in their designated groups.

3. Ask students to explain how they acted like scientists. *(We put things that were made the same into groups. We named the groups.)*

4. Using page 20, students sort items into natural and manmade groups.

5. Have students add classroom items to the two groups.

Natural or Manmade?

Scientists put things in groups. We put things in groups, too.

Is It Magnetic?

Materials (for each group)

- magnet
- nail
- eraser
- crayon
- metal key
- rubber band
- paper clip
- cork
- metal scissors
- feather
- two plastic plates

- record sheet on page 21, reproduced for each student

Steps to Follow

1. Divide the class into small groups. Give each group a box containing the items listed above.

2. Ask students to recall what they know about magnets. Then ask them to divide the objects into two groups: things they predict will be attracted to the magnet and things they think will not.

3. Students on each team take turns using their magnet to divide the objects into two groups. They then complete their record sheets.

4. Ask students to explain how they have acted like scientists. Use questioning to help students clarify their ideas. *(We put things that are alike together.)*

5. Have each group share their results. Put all the objects that were picked up together on a table. Ask, "How are these all the same? What did we learn about magnets?" *(Magnets pick up metal objects.)* Ask, "What can we name this group?" *(Things a magnet can pick up. Magnetic things.)* Have students put the remaining items together and give the group a name. *(Things a magnet won't pick up. Things that are not magnetic.)*

6. Place completed record sheets in students' logbooks.

7. Record student responses to the questions in steps 4 and 5 on a chart entitled "Magnets."

8. Students are to locate other magnetic items around the classroom.

page 21

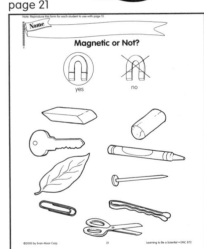

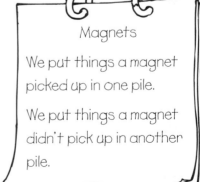

Magnets

We put things a magnet picked up in one pile.

We put things a magnet didn't pick up in another pile.

Sorting Materials

Materials (for each group)

At least four small objects made of each of these materials:

- plastic—(e.g., drinking straw, plastic cup, plastic spoon, Unifix® cubes)
- metal—(e.g., can, washer, nuts and bolts, foil)
- wood—(e.g., toothpick, craft stick, wooden block, wooden spoon)
- aluminum pie pan
- plastic plate
- shallow wooden bowl or tray
- record sheet on page 22, reproduced for each student

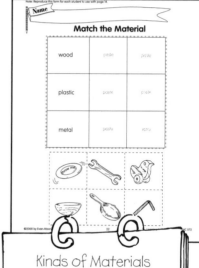

page 22

Steps to Follow

1. Show students a collection of plates—a metal pie pan, a plastic plate, and a wooden bowl or tray. Ask, "What is this plate made of?" Label each of the plates. Ask students to think of other objects that are made of the same material as the plate shown.

2. Divide the class into small groups. Give each group one each of the sorting plates and a selection of items to sort.

   Students place each of their items on the plate that is made of the same type of material. After the sorting is completed, ask students to describe how all of the objects of one material are alike. Ask, "What is the name of this set?"

3. Ask students to explain how they have been scientists. *(We put things that are alike on the same plate. We thought about how things go together. We named the groups.)* Record student responses to steps 2 and 3 on a chart.

4. Using page 22, students paste items into the correct categories.

Kinds of Materials

We put wooden things together. We put plastic things together. We put metal things together. We named our groups.

Include these pages in each student's logbook.

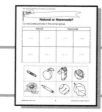

bear cub

Learning to Be a Scientist • EMC 872

duck

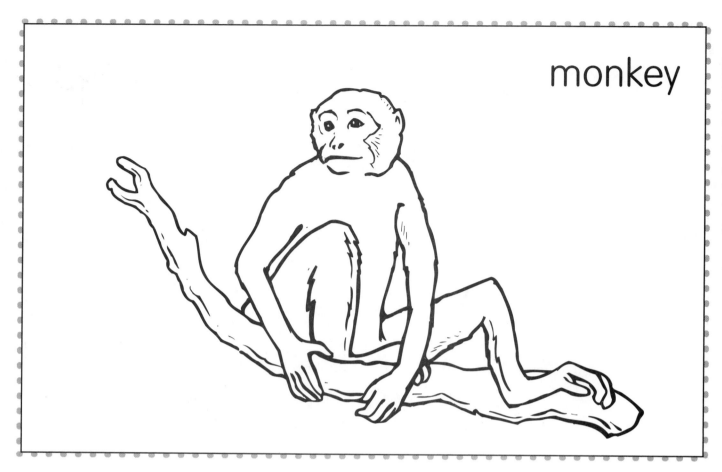

monkey

Learning to Be a Scientist • EMC 872

hen

dog

17

penguin

cat

Learning to Be a Scientist • EMC 872

robin

mouse

Learning to Be a Scientist • EMC 872

turkey

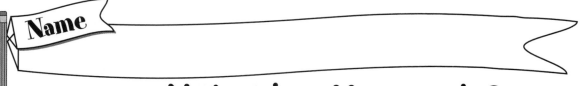

Name

Natural or Manmade?

Cut and paste pictures in the correct group.

Natural		Manmade	
paste	paste	paste	paste
paste	paste	paste	paste

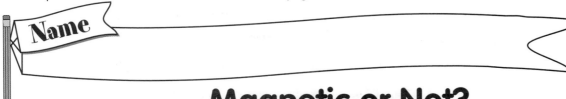

Magnetic or Not?

yes

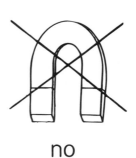
no

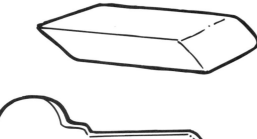

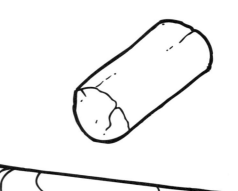

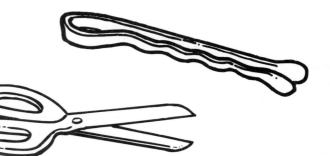

Match the Material

wood	paste	paste
plastic	paste	paste
metal	paste	paste

Learning to Be a Scientist • EMC 872

Let's Look for Materials!

1. Cut on the -------------- line.
2. Put the pages in 1-2-3 order.
3. Staple the corner and take the book home.
4. Do the work and bring the book back to school.

1

My Little Book of Materials

Name

©2000 by Evan-Moor Corp. • EMC 872

2

This is made of plastic.

©2000 by Evan-Moor Corp. • EMC 872

3

This is made of wood.

©2000 by Evan-Moor Corp. • EMC 872

4

This is made of metal.

©2000 by Evan-Moor Corp. • EMC 872

5

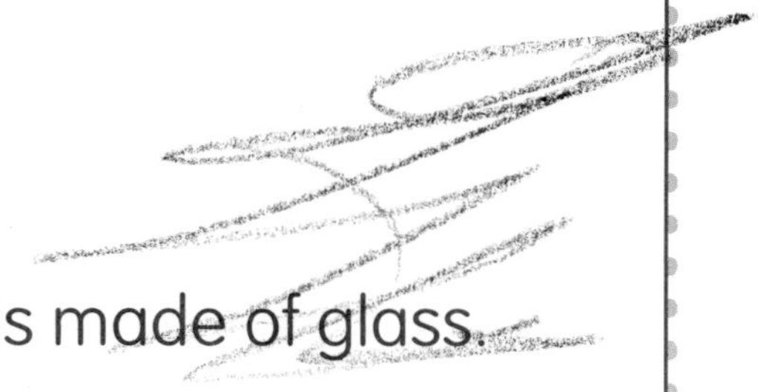

This is made of glass.

6

This is made of paper.

©2000 by Evan-Moor Corp. • EMC 872

7

This is made of cloth.

©2000 by Evan-Moor Corp. • EMC 872

8

This is made of more than one material.

©2000 by Evan-Moor Corp. • EMC 872

9

I don't know what this is made out of.

©2000 by Evan-Moor Corp. • EMC 872

Dear Parents,

We are learning about the different materials out of which things are made. Help your child complete this little book by having a materials hunt around the house. Your child is to draw or write on each page to show what was found.

Sincerely,

©2000 by Evan-Moor Corp. • EMC 872

Scientists make comparisons.

Making a Comparison

- Explain that scientists often ask how things are alike and how they are different. Show students two toy animals. Ask them to tell how the animals are alike. Then have them tell how the animals are different. Explain that what they are doing is comparing. Say, "Now you are going to be scientists as you compare things."

- In the following three activities, students will practice making comparisons.

Comparing Animals

Materials

- picture cards on pages 28–33
- record sheets on pages 34 and 35, reproduced for each student

Steps to Follow

1. Read *Big & Little* by Steve Jenkins. Students compare the two animals on each page, describing how they are different (each time one is obviously larger than the other). List the animals shown on a chart under two headings—"Large Animals" and "Small Animals."

2. Display the picture cards, asking students to decide which animals belong in the large set and which belong in the small set.

3. Then display all of the cards and ask students to think of another way the animals can be compared (by body covering, number of legs, how they move, etc.).

   Ask students to explain how they are acting as scientists. Use questioning to help them verbalize what they have done. *(We are deciding how things are alike and how they are different. We are comparing things.)* Add their responses to the animal chart.

4. Using page 34, students review the concept of large and small.

5. Each student finds one large object and one small object in the classroom. Using page 35, students draw the objects.

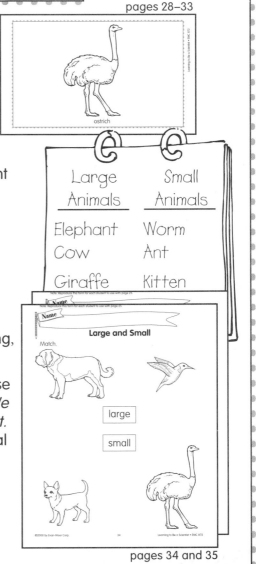

pages 28–33

pages 34 and 35

Will It Bend?

Materials (for each student)

- paper bag
- drinking straw
- tongue depressor
- pipe cleaner
- pencil
- paper clip
- file card
- record sheet on page 36, reproduced for each student

page 36

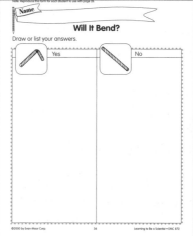

Steps to Follow

1. Show each item listed above. Ask students to name the items. Provide any names they do not know. List the names on the chalkboard to help students in completing their record sheet.

2. Give each student a bag containing the objects listed above and a copy of the record sheet.

3. Students are to sort the objects into two groups—those that bend and those that do not bend. (Emphasize that breaking in half is not the same as bending.)

   Students draw or write the name of each object in the correct box on the record sheet.

4. Ask students to describe how they are acting like scientists. Use questioning to help students synthesize an answer. *(We are comparing what things can do. We are finding out how things are alike and how they are different.)*

   Record the results of the comparison on a chart for the class logbook.

5. Ask students to think of things they use that need to bend. Then ask, "Are there some things that you use that shouldn't bend?"

Will It Bend?

Some things would bend.

Some things would not bend.

Some things broke.

Which Is Easier?

Materials

- cardboard box
- classroom objects (books, lunch boxes, etc.)
- wagon
- record sheet on page 37, reproduced for each student

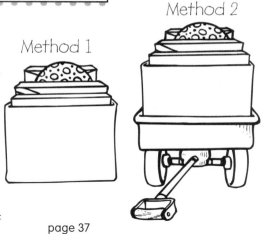

Method 1

Method 2

Steps to Follow

1. Fill the box with classroom objects. Make it heavy but not impossible for students to move with effort. Explain to students that they are going to compare two ways of moving the box.

2. Select several students to take turns trying to push the cardboard box across the floor. Have an adult put the box in the wagon, and then have the same students pull the wagon containing the cardboard box across the floor. Have the remainder of the students observe what is happening.

3. Ask students to tell what was the same each time. *(We had to move a box full of stuff.)* Ask them to tell what was different. *(One time the box was on the floor. One time it was in the wagon.)*

4. Ask students to compare the two methods they used.

   Method 1—*We pushed the box on the floor. It was hard to push the box on the floor. The box was too heavy to push. We couldn't move it very far.*

   Method 2—*We pushed the box in the wagon. It was easier to move the box with the wagon. We could move it as far as we wanted to.*

5. Ask students to explain how they are acting like scientists. *(We are comparing things. We are trying different ways to see how they are different.)* Write their responses on a chart for the class logbook.

6. Using page 37, students record the results of the experiment.

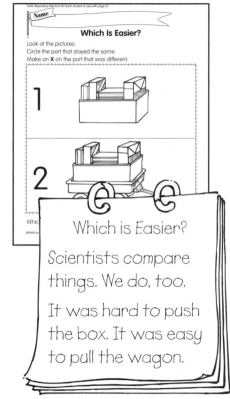

page 37

Which Is Easier?

Look at the pictures.
Circle the part that stayed the same.
Make an **X** on the part that was different.

Which is Easier?

Scientists compare things. We do, too.

It was hard to push the box. It was easy to pull the wagon.

**Logbook**

Include these pages in each student's logbook.

ostrich

Learning to Be a Scientist • EMC 872

hummingbird

rhino

pig

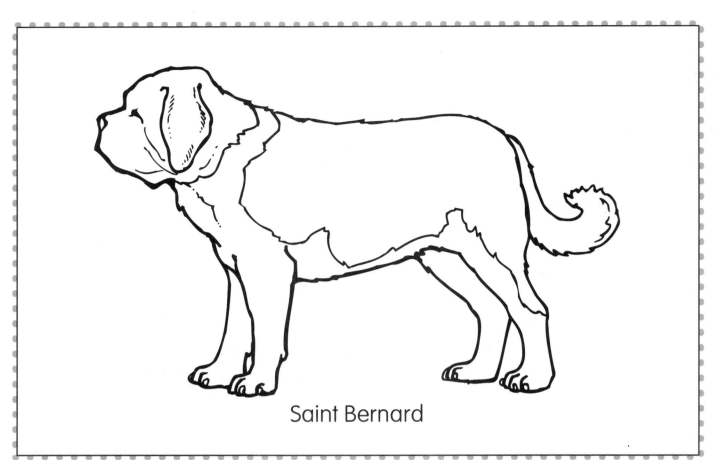

Saint Bernard

Learning to Be a Scientist • EMC 872

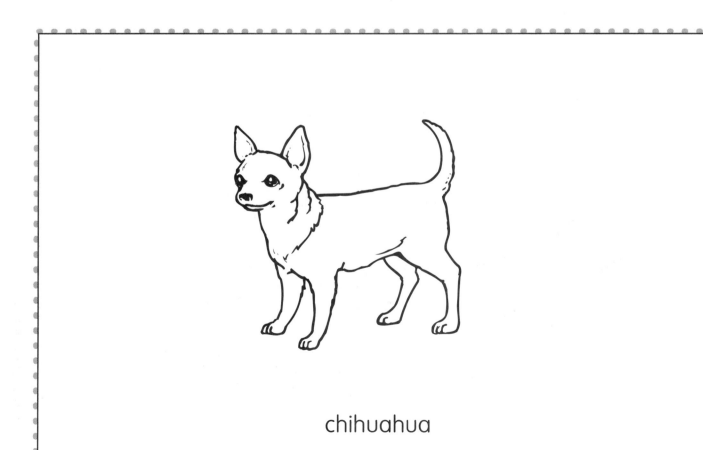

chihuahua

monkey

gorilla

goldfish

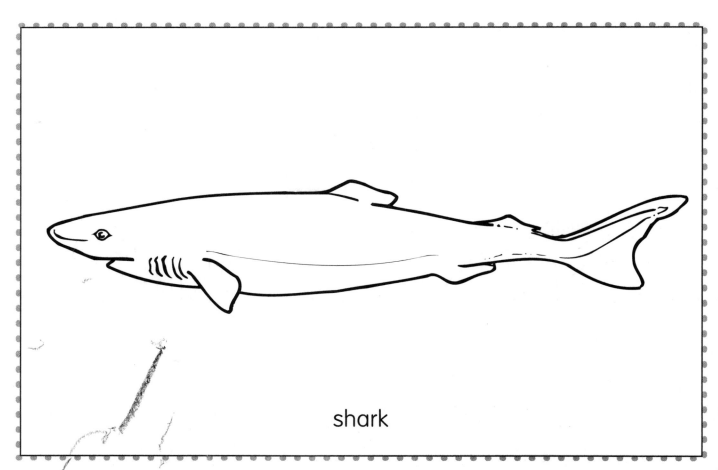

shark

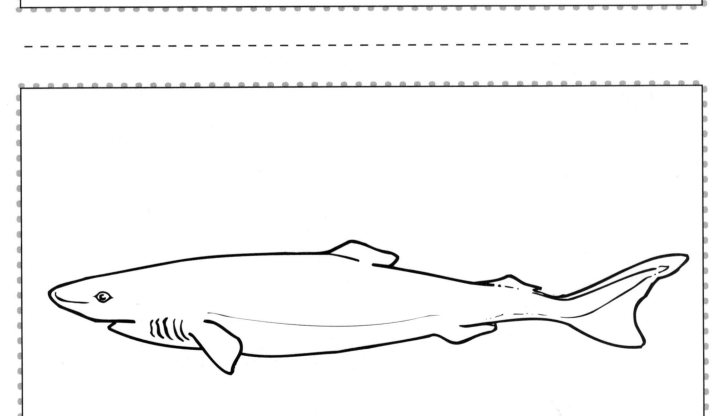

goldfish

shark

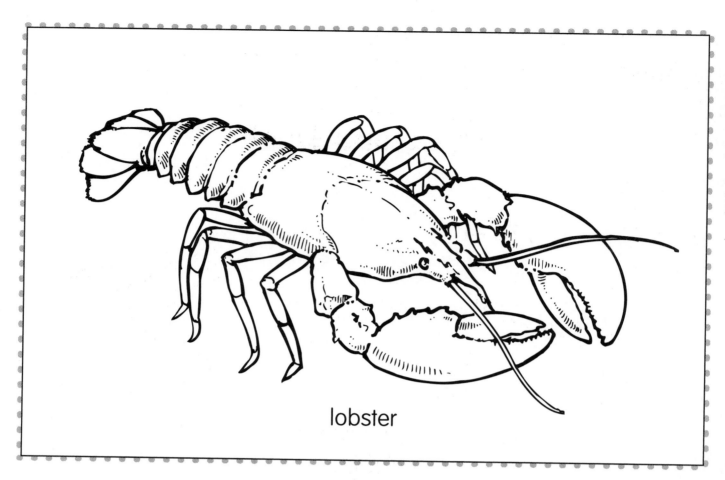

lobster

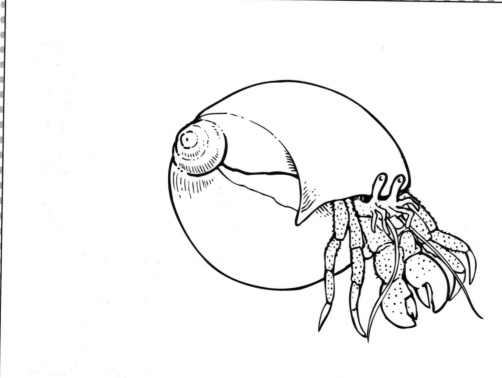

hermit crab

Learning to Be a Scientist • EMC 872

Name

Large and Small

Match.

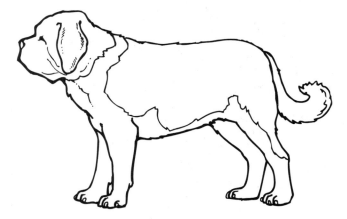

large

small

Large and Small

Look around the classroom.

Find something large.
Draw it here.

Find something small.
Draw it here.

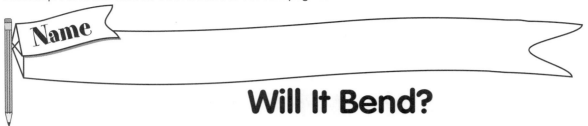

Name

Will It Bend?

Draw or list your answers.

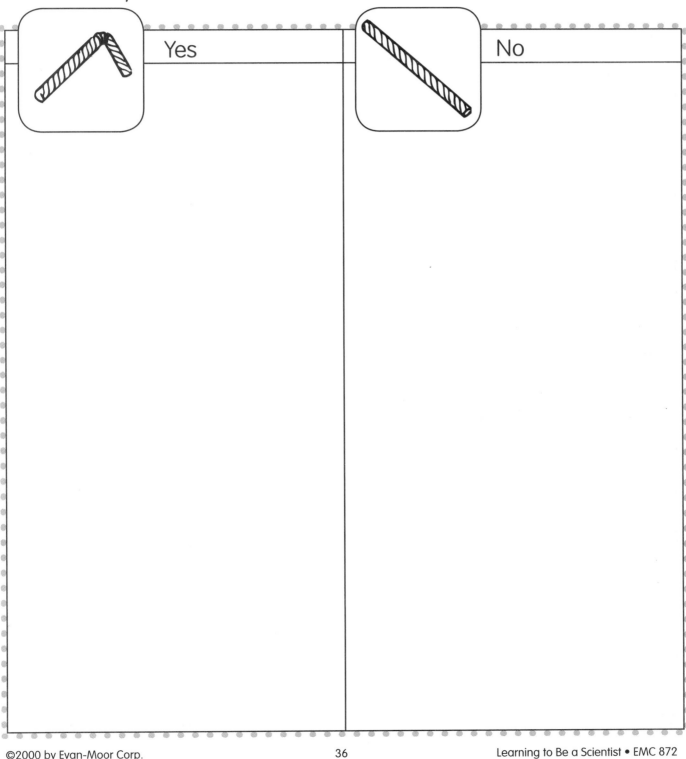

Yes	No

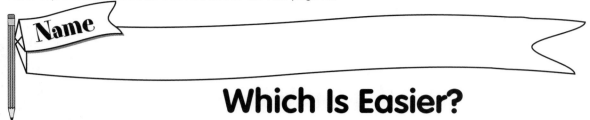

Name

Which Is Easier?

Look at the pictures.

Circle the part that stayed the same.

Make an **X** on the part that was different.

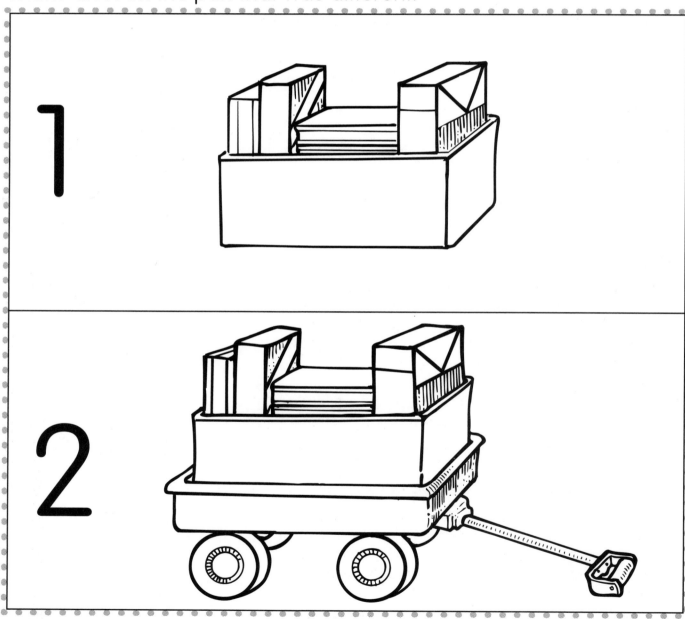

1

2

Which was easier?　　1　　　2

Scientists make measurements.

Making Measurements

- Explain that scientists measure things to find out about them. Demonstrate measurement by measuring the height of one student. Say, "You are going to be scientists as you measure things in different ways."

- In the following three activities, students will be making various types of measurements.

Hotter or Colder?

Materials

- thermometer with large numerals

- three glasses of water—room temperature, water with ice, heated water

- record sheets on pages 41 and 42, reproduced for each student

pages 41 and 42

Steps to Follow

1. Students look at a thermometer set in a glass of room-temperature water to see where the colored line reaches. (Some students may be ready to read the nearest number.) Show students how to color the first thermometer on their record sheet to show the temperature.

2. Place the thermometer in a glass of ice water. Ask students to tell what they see. *(The colored line went down.)* Use questioning to help students explain that the line goes down because the water is colder than in the first glass. Have students color the second thermometer on their record sheet.

3. Repeat the same steps with the glass of hot water.

4. Ask students to explain how they acted like scientists. *(We measured to learn about how hot or cold the water was. We used a thermometer.)* Have them refer to their record sheet as they explain what they learned about measuring temperature. Record their responses on a chart.

5. Using page 42, students mark the different kinds of thermometers being used. Place completed record sheets in students' logbooks.

How Big Is It?

Materials (for pairs of students)

- a large oval or round rock
- string
- marking pen
- balance scale
- Unifix® cubes or small blocks
- record sheet on page 43, reproduced for each student
- minibook on pages 44–46, reproduced for each student

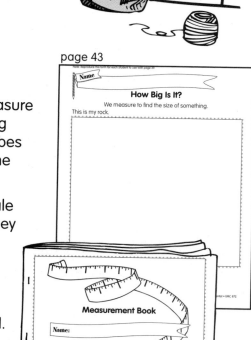

page 43

Steps to Follow

1. Working in pairs, students use a piece of string to measure around the rock. They mark the string with the marking pen. Then they lay the string down and use Unifix® cubes or small blocks to see how long the string is. Record the results on their record sheets in "number of blocks."

2. Students place their rock on one side of a balance scale and small blocks on the other side until it balances. They count the number of blocks and record the results in "number of blocks."

3. Ask students to explain how they are acting like scientists. *(We are measuring our rocks to find out about them.)* Then have them share what they learned. Use the information to help the class determine who has the biggest rock and who has the heaviest rock.

   Record student responses on a chart.

4. Place completed record sheets in students' logbooks.

5. Using pages 44–46, students work with a partner to complete a minibook containing some of their own measurements.

   Give each student four pieces of string 24" (61 cm) long and a marking pen. They are to measure and mark the string as they did in step one. If your students are ready, provide a cloth measuring tape for each pair of students.

pages 44–46

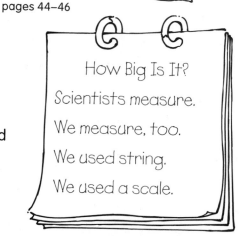

How Big Is It?
Scientists measure.
We measure, too.
We used string.
We used a scale.

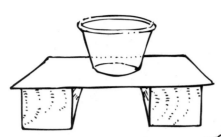

Materials (for each group)

- two index cards—5" x 7" (13 x 18 cm), one flat and one accordion-folded

- a clear plastic cup

- a handful of small pebbles or washers

- two building blocks

- record sheet on page 47, reproduced for each student

Which is Stronger?

Scientists measure.

We measure, too.

We measured our bridges. The folded one was stronger.

Steps to Follow

1. Ask students, "How can you show the class that you are strong?" *(I can lift something heavy. I can make a big muscle with my arm.)*

   Explain that it is possible to test how strong something is. Show two "bridges"—one made with a flat index card and one made with an accordion-folded card (place the blocks about 5" [13 cm] apart). Students predict which bridge is stronger.

2. Divide students into small groups. They first build a bridge with the flat card, then place a cup on the bridge. They test the bridge by adding pebbles to the cup until the bridge collapses. Record the number of pebbles used.

   Repeat the process using the accordion-folded card.

   page 47

3. Ask students to explain how they are acting like scientists. *(We are measuring things. We are seeing which bridge can hold the most rocks.)* Then have groups compare their results. Ask questions such as, "Which bridge was stronger? How do you know it is stronger?"

   Record student responses on a chart entitled "Which Bridge was Stronger?"

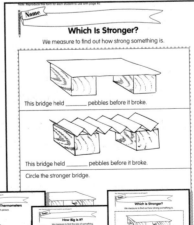

Logbook

Include these pages in each student's logbook.

Name

Hotter or Colder?

A thermometer measures how hot something is.

1

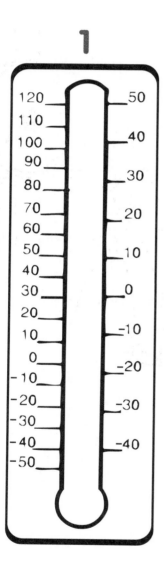

2

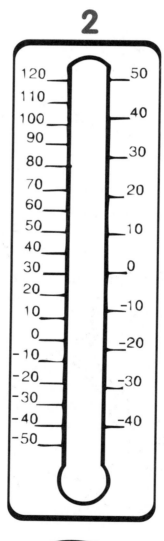

3

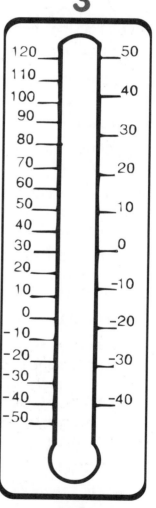

Find the Thermometers

Circle the thermometer in each picture.

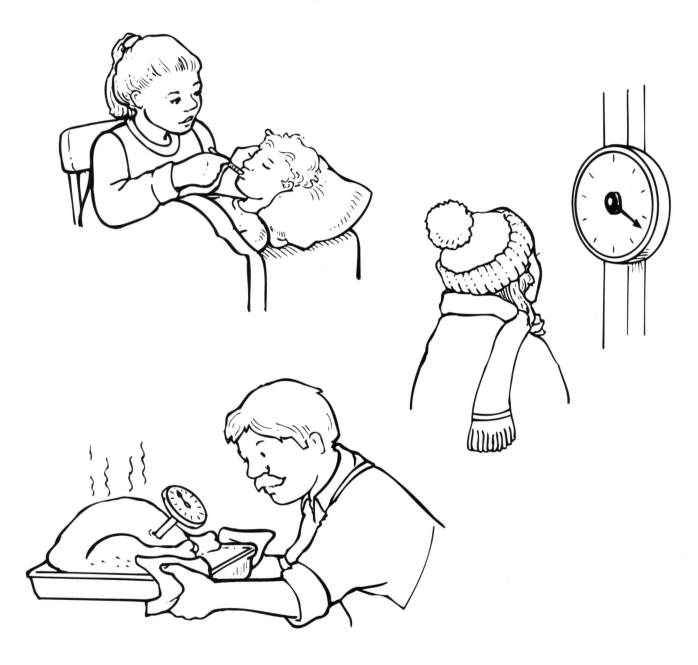

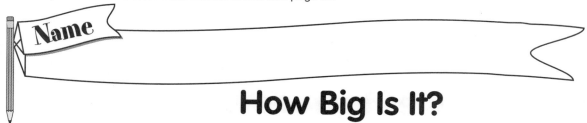

Name

How Big Is It?

We measure to find the size of something.

This is my rock.

It is _____ around.

It weighs _____.

Learning to Be a Scientist • EMC 872

Measurement Book

Name:

My head is _____ around.

2

My waist is _____ around.

3

- -

My wrist is _____ around.

4

My foot is _____ long.

5

_____ helped measure me.
(helper's name)

Draw what you used to measure your body.

6

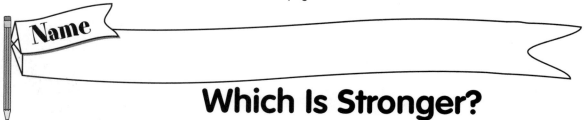

Which Is Stronger?

We measure to find out how strong something is.

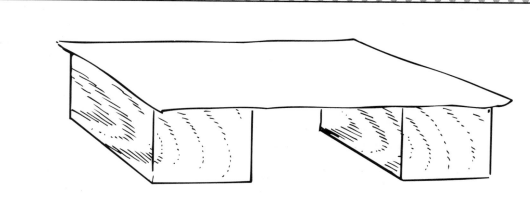

This bridge held _____ pebbles before it broke.

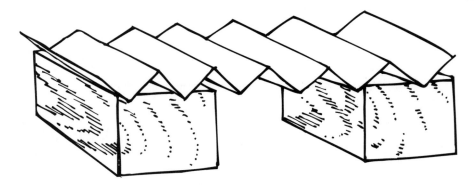

This bridge held _____ pebbles before it broke.

Circle the stronger bridge.

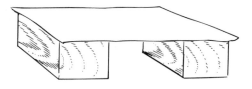
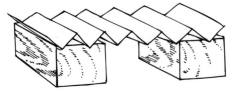

Scientists use tools and equipment.

Tools and Equipment

- Explain that scientists use many kinds of tools and equipment when they do investigations. Read and discuss the minibook on pages 51–53. Then show an assortment of tools your young scientists might use (e.g., hand lens, balance scale, funnel and container, small pulley, scissors). Discuss how each piece of equipment might be used. Say, "Now you are going to be using different kinds of tools and equipment."

- In the following three activities, students will identify and use different types of tools.

Choosing the Right Tool

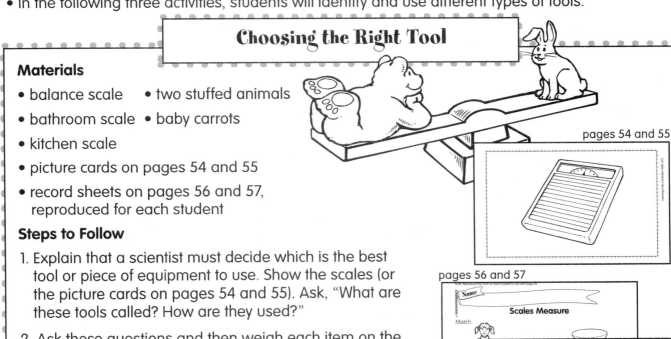

Materials

- balance scale
- two stuffed animals
- bathroom scale
- baby carrots
- kitchen scale
- picture cards on pages 54 and 55
- record sheets on pages 56 and 57, reproduced for each student

pages 54 and 55

pages 56 and 57

Scales Measure

Choose the Right Tool

The Right Tool
Scientists pick the right tool.
We picked the right tool, too.

Steps to Follow

1. Explain that a scientist must decide which is the best tool or piece of equipment to use. Show the scales (or the picture cards on pages 54 and 55). Ask, "What are these tools called? How are they used?"

2. Ask these questions and then weigh each item on the scale chosen. Students complete page 56.

    "Look at these two stuffed animals. I want to know which one is heavier. Which scale should I use? Why?"

    "Which scale should I use to find out how much (child's name) weighs? Why?"

    "I need three pounds of these apples. Which scale should I use? Why?"

3. Ask students to explain how they are acting like scientists. *(We are using tools. We are picking the right thing to use.)* Ask them to name the tools they used.

    Record student responses on a chart for the class log.

4. Students complete page 57.

Take a Closer Look

Materials (for each student)

- hand lens

- small object to observe—leaf, insect, earthworm, etc.

- crayons

- record sheets on pages 58 and 59, reproduced for each student

- overhead transparency of page 59

Steps to Follow

1. Show students a hand lens. Ask them to give its name *(magnifying glass* or *hand lens)* and tell how it is used. Ask, "When would a scientist use a magnifying glass or hand lens?" *(to make something look bigger)* Explain to students that they will be using hand lenses to take a closer look at things, too.

2. Provide each student with a hand lens, a small object or creature to look at, and a record sheet. They are to look at their object with their eyes and draw what they see on the record sheet.

   They then look at the object with the hand lens and draw what they see.

   Place completed drawings in students' logbooks.

3. Ask students to describe what they have done and what they learned.

   Ask, "What have you done that a scientist might do?" *(We used a tool to look at something. We used a tool to make something look bigger.)* Ask students to name the tool they used.

   Record student responses to step 3 on a class chart.

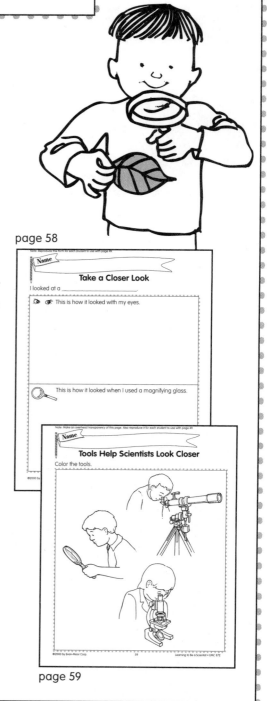

page 58

page 59

Making Connections

Make an overhead transparency of page 59. Point to each picture and ask students to name the tool being used. Provide the names they cannot provide. Ask students to explain why the scientist is using that tool *(to make things look bigger; to take a closer look)*. Give each student a copy of the page. Have them color each of the tools.

Reflections

Materials

- hand mirror
- ball
- flashlight
- unbreakable mirrors
- record sheet on page 60, reproduced for each student

page 60

Steps to Follow

1. Before students arrive, set up a mirror so that it reflects a very bright spot of sunlight on an easily noticed location. When students notice the spot of light, ask them what they think is causing it. Use questioning to help them clarify that the spot of light is coming from the mirror. Explain that the sunlight from outside is bouncing off the mirror.

2. Give each student a mirror. Challenge them to use their mirrors to make spots of light on the ceiling or wall.

3. Use a ball to demonstrate what is happening to the light. Bounce a ball straight against a wall and catch it as it returns to you. Explain to students that light is like the ball. Light bounces off surfaces and travels back the same way it came unless something gets in the way. The bouncing back of a ray of light from a surface is called *reflection*.

4. Darken the room and beam a flashlight on a mirror at an angle. Have students compare the ball and the light beam.

5. Ask students to describe what they learned. *(Light bounces back. A mirror reflects light.)* Ask them to name the tools and equipment they used (mirrors, ball, flashlight). Ask them to explain how they have been acting like scientists. *(We used tools to find out about light.)*

   Record their observations on a chart.

6. Using page 60, students draw rays of light to show the direction in which they move.

Include these pages in each student's logbook.

Scientists at Work

Name: _____

1

Scientists use tools and equipment.

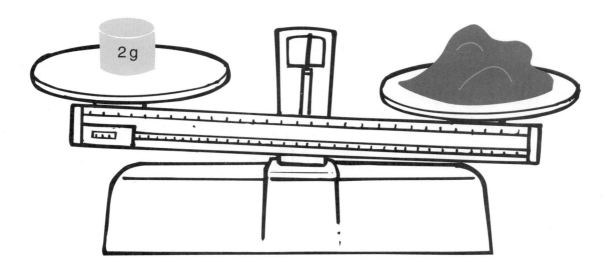

2g

2

They use tools to look
at things far away.

3

They use tools to
make small
things look bigger.

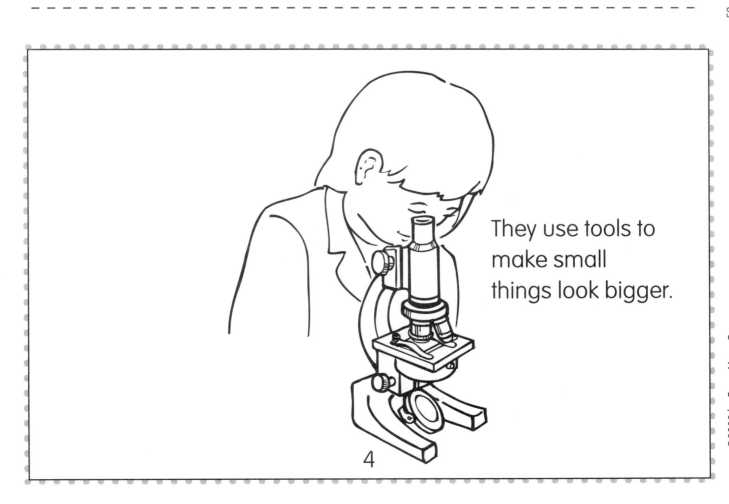

4

They use tools to put things together and take them apart.

5

We use tools, too.

6

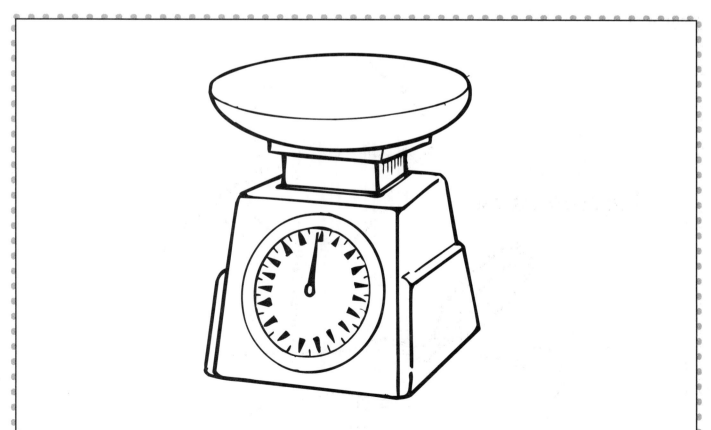

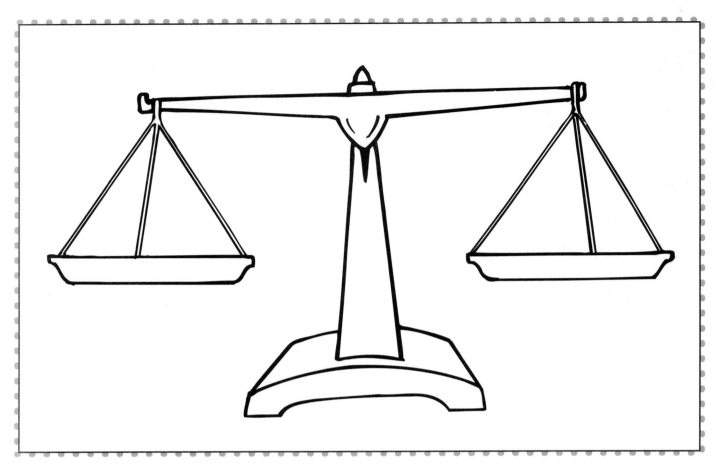

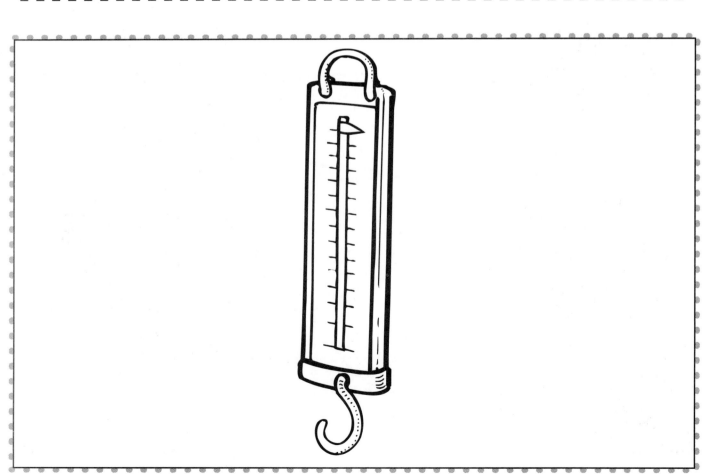

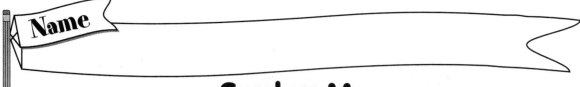

Name

Scales Measure

Match.

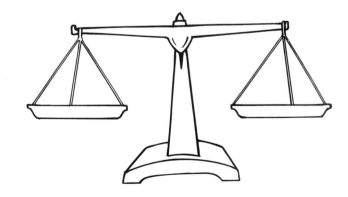

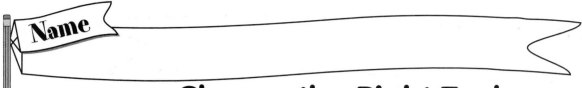

Name

Choose the Right Tool

Match.

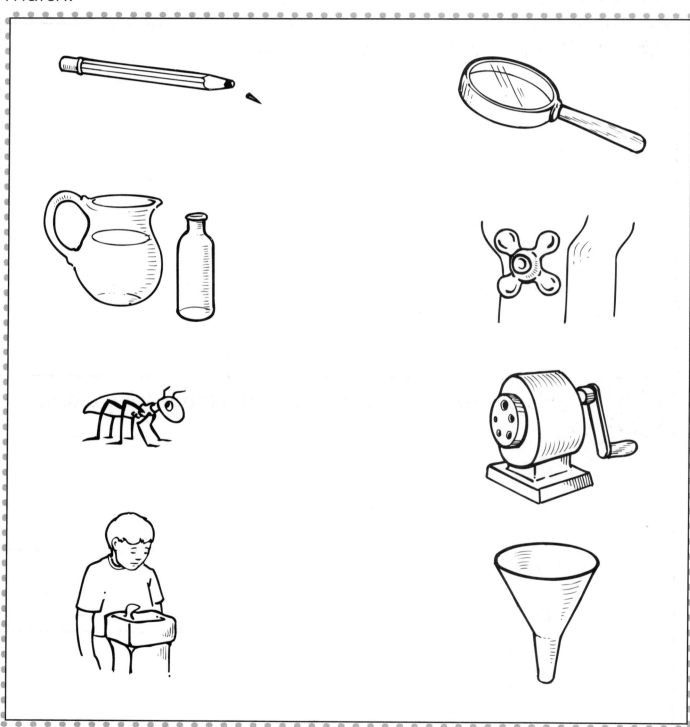

 **Name**

Take a Closer Look

I looked at a _____.

 👁 This is how it looked with my eyes.

 This is how it looked when I used a magnifying glass.

Name

Tools Help Scientists Look Closer

Color the tools.

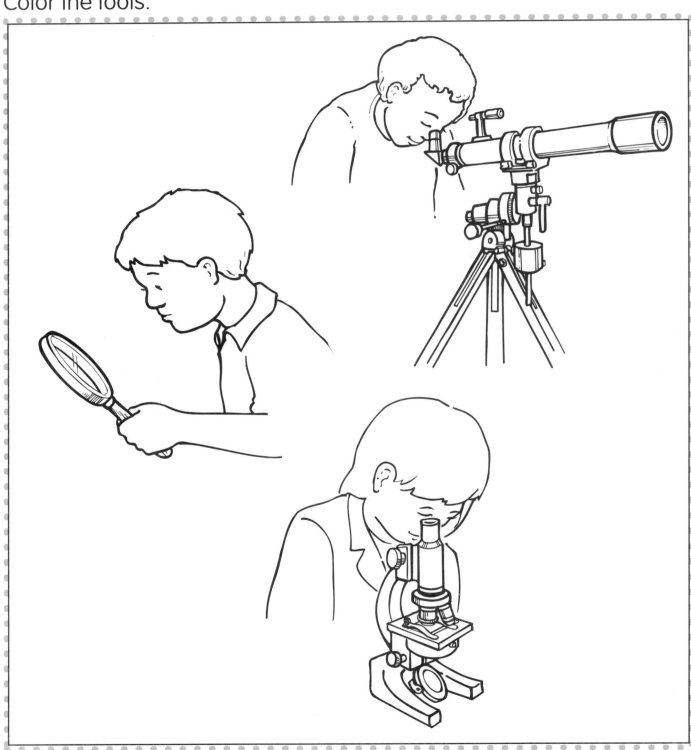

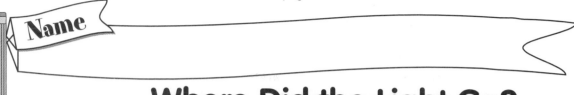

Where Did the Light Go?

Draw the light's path.

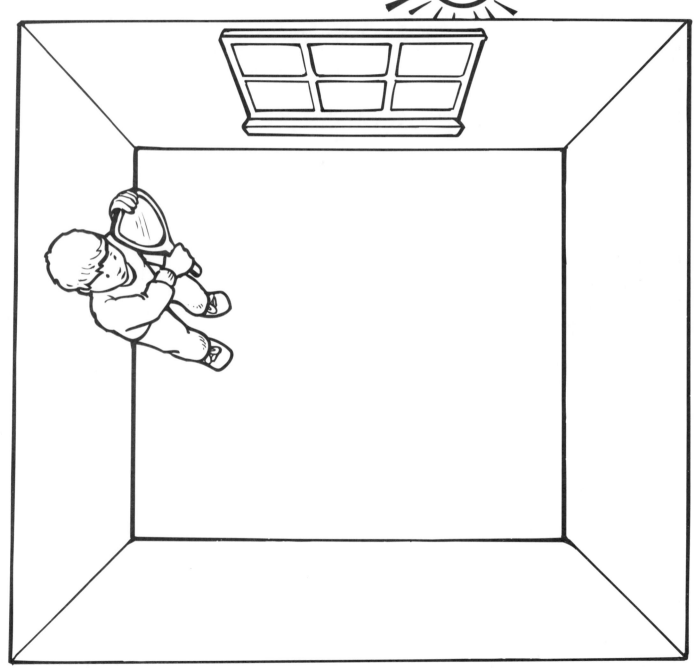

Scientists record information and explain it to others.

Recording and Explaining Information

- Read and discuss a nonfiction animal book with your students. (*What Do You Do When Something Wants to Eat You?* by Steve Jenkins and *These Birds Can't Fly* by Allan Fowler are good examples of books you could use.) Students share orally what they learned.

  Say, "You listened to a story about animals. Then you talked about what you learned from the story. Sharing information with others is one thing scientists do. Scientists must remember what they discover (recording information), and they must share what they learn with other people (explaining). You are going to learn how to record what you discover and then share what you learn with the rest of the class."

- In the following five activities, students will be recording information in various ways.

Making a List

Materials (for each student)

- clipboard with pencil attached (see page 4)

Steps to Follow

1. Explain that sometimes scientists make lists of what they observe. Give each student a clipboard. Go for a short walk through the school and around the school yard. Students are to listen for sounds. They are to draw or list each thing they hear.

2. Back in the classroom, have each student share one or more sounds he or she heard. Record these on the chalkboard.

3. Ask students to explain how they are acting like scientists. Guide them to verbalize that they recorded information in a list and that they shared the list with others.

   Record their responses on a chart entitled "Record and Explain."

Record and Explain

1. We made a list of sounds we heard.

2.

Making a Model

Explain that sometimes scientists make models of what they observe to share with others. Students will make a model of an animal.

Materials

- nonfiction animal books
- self-hardening clay
- cardboard
- white glue
- black marking pens

Steps to Follow

1. Share nonfiction picture books containing photographs of animals. (Use books such as *Box Turtle at Long Pond* by William T. George and *African Elephants* by Roland Smith, which have clear photographs of animals.) Discuss the various external parts of different animals.

2. Each student selects an animal and makes a clay model of it.

3. After the clay hardens, glue it onto a sturdy piece of cardboard. Write the name of the animal on the cardboard.

4. Have each student share his or her animal model with the class, pointing out the external parts and relating any information known about how the part is used.

5. Ask students to explain how they acted like scientists. *(We made models of animals to show the parts. We shared what we know about the animal.)*

   Add their responses to the "Record and Explain" chart.

Record and Explain

1. We made a list of sounds we heard.

2. We made models of animals to show the parts.

Making a Graph

Materials (for each student)

- paper sack

- assorted seeds—3 to 6 kinds of seeds; varying amounts, but no more than 9 of a kind

- glue

- record sheet on page 66, reproduced for each student

Steps to Follow

1. Explain that sometimes scientists graph information they have observed. Ask your students to recall graphs they have made in class. Ask, "What did the graph show? What did we do with the graph?"

2. Give each student a sack of seeds. (Have a different number of seeds in each sack.) Explain that they will be making a graph to record information about the seeds in their sacks. Model how this will be done.

    a. Separate the seeds by kind.

    b. Glue each kind of seed in a separate column—one seed to a box.

3. Divide the class into small groups. Have students share their graphs with their group.

4. As a class, ask students to tell what they know from reading the graph. *(I can see that George had three pumpkin seeds. I had more sunflower seeds than beans.)* Post the completed graphs on a bulletin board for everyone to see.

5. Ask students to explain how they acted like scientists. Use questioning to help them express what they did. *(We found out what was in our sacks. We counted and made a graph. We showed our graphs to other people.)*

    Add student responses to the "Record and Explain" chart.

page 66

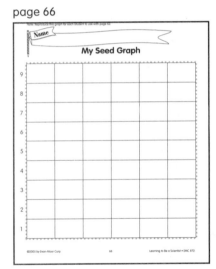

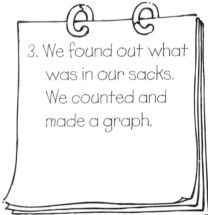

3. We found out what was in our sacks. We counted and made a graph.

Making a Diagram

Materials (for each student)

- sheet of drawing paper
- crayons
- overhead transparency of page 70

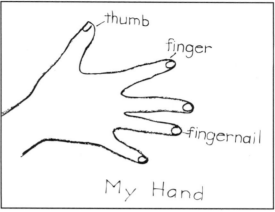

My Hand

Steps to Follow

1. Explain that a diagram is a drawing of something with the different parts labeled. Show the overhead transparency of the apple diagram. As students name the parts, label the stem, peel, flesh, core, and seeds. Explain that they are going to look carefully at their own hand and then diagram it.

2. Have students place a hand on the drawing paper and trace around it. (Students may work in pairs to assist each other in this step.) They then add details to the diagram, for example, knuckles, fingernails, freckles, scratches, etc., that make the diagram uniquely theirs.

   Help students label their diagrams by listing words they might need on the chalkboard.

3. Divide the class into groups. Mix up the diagrams for each group and pass them out to group members. Each student uses the details in the picture to try to match the diagram to the correct person. Ask students to explain how they were able to find the correct person. *(I knew it was Jose's hand because it had a scratch on it. Kim's hand has freckles on it.)*

4. Ask students to explain how they acted like scientists. Use questioning to help them express what they did. *(We looked at our hands and drew a picture. We put names by the parts. We looked at the pictures to find out things.)*

   Record student responses on the "Record and Explain" chart.

page 70

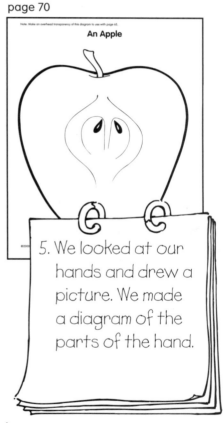

5. We looked at our hands and drew a picture. We made a diagram of the parts of the hand.

Logbook

Include this page in each student's logbook.

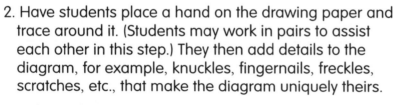

Name

My Seed Graph

9					
8					
7					
6					
5					
4					
3					
2					
1					

Learning to Be a Scientist • EMC 872

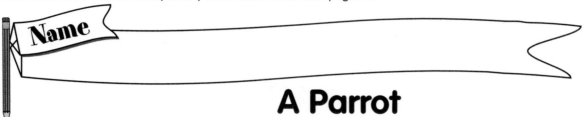

A Parrot

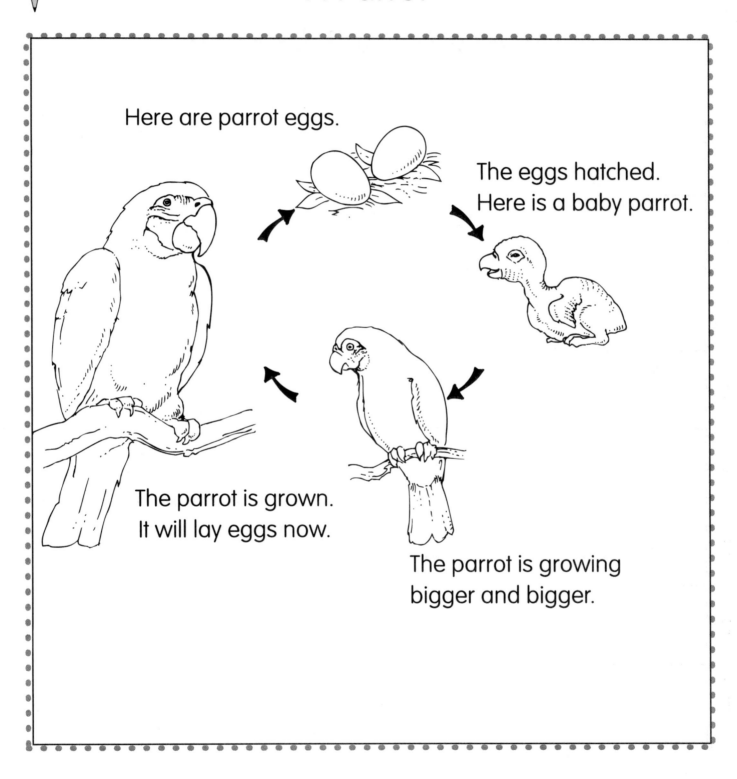

Here are parrot eggs.

The eggs hatched.
Here is a baby parrot.

The parrot is grown.
It will lay eggs now.

The parrot is growing
bigger and bigger.

Pumpkin Chart Patterns

A Pumpkin Grows

This is a pumpkin flower.
It will grow into a pumpkin.

This is a pumpkin plant.
It will grow bigger
and bigger.

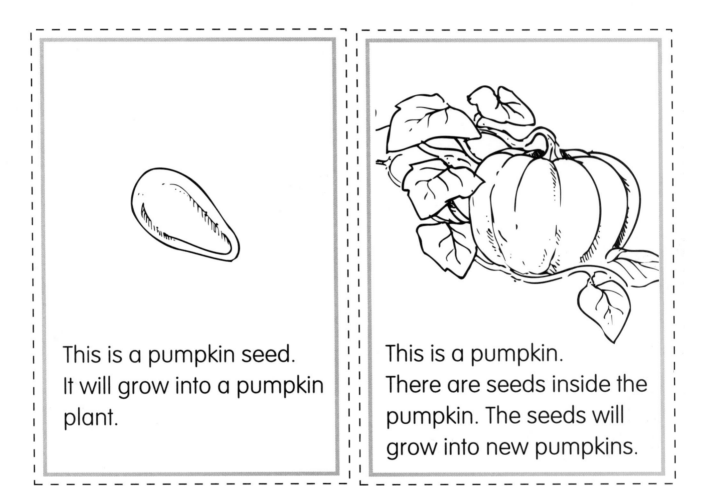

This is a pumpkin seed.
It will grow into a pumpkin plant.

This is a pumpkin.
There are seeds inside the pumpkin. The seeds will grow into new pumpkins.

Learning to Be a Scientist • EMC 872

An Apple

　　　　　　70　　　　　　Learning to Be a Scientist • EMC 872

Scientists conduct investigations.

Conducting an Investigation

- Explain that when scientists want to learn about things, they do experiments to find out what will happen. These are called *investigations*. Ask students to recall the things scientists do that they have learned to do *(watch what happens, use tools, record what they see, sort and name categories, compare, and measure)*. Whenever a scientist does an investigation, he or she does all these things.

  Say, "Now you are going to be scientists again. You are going to investigate to see what you can find out about magnets."

- In the following three investigations, students will be using the process skills practiced in the other sections of *Learning to Be a Scientist*.

Will a Magnet Work Through Other Materials?

Students will discover that a magnet will be attracted to metal through some materials but not others.

Materials (for each student)

- paper clip
- magnet
- plastic cup
- tongue depressor or craft stick
- sheet of paper
- scrap of cloth
- record sheet on page 75, reproduced for each student

Learning to Be a Scientist • EMC 872

Steps to Follow

1. Show the various materials (plastic cup, paper, cotton cloth, wooden stick) and have students predict which materials a magnet will work through. Record predictions on the chalkboard.

2. Students follow these oral directions:

   a. Put a paper clip in your cup. Move the magnet along the outside of the cup. Did the magnet attract the paper clip? Mark your answer, "yes" or "no," on the record sheet.

   b. Put the paper clip under the sheet of paper. Place the magnet on the paper. Did the magnet attract the paper clip through the paper? Mark your answer.

   c. Put the paper clip under the piece of cloth. Place the magnet on top of the cloth. Did the magnet attract the paper clip through the cloth? Mark your answer.

   d. Put the paper clip on top of the wooden stick. Hold the stick and put the magnet under it. Move the magnet to see if you can get the paper clip to move. Mark your answer.

3. Ask students to share what they discovered. (*My magnet pulled the paper clip in the plastic cup. My magnet didn't move the paper clip when it was under the stick.*) Ask them to explain why this happened.

page 75

4. Ask students to tell how they acted like scientists. (*We did an experiment. We watched to see what happened. We used tools. We marked what we saw on our papers. We told what happened.*)

   Record student responses to steps 3 and 4 on a chart.

   Place completed record sheets in students' logbooks.

5. As a follow-up, have students look for other items to use and repeat the experiment (glass container, cardboard, heavier and thinner cloth, etc.).

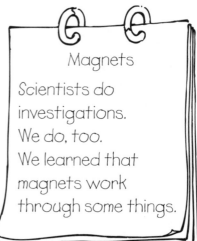

Magnets
Scientists do investigations. We do, too. We learned that magnets work through some things.

Do Oil and Water Mix?

Materials (for each student)

- vegetable oil
- food coloring
- water
- spoon
- jar with a lid
- record sheet on page 76, reproduced for each student

page 76

Steps to Follow

1. Show students a container of oil and one of water. Ask them to predict what will happen if the two are mixed together. Will they mix or not?

2. Students fill their jars half full of water and add three drops of food coloring. They add five spoonfuls of oil to the colored water. Then they put the lid on the jar and shake it. Place the jar on the table and watch to see what happens.

3. Using page 76, students record what they observed. Discuss their observations as a class. *(The oil didn't mix with the water. The oil floated on top.)* Explain that this is because oil is lighter (less dense) than water.

4. Ask students to recall how they acted like scientists. *(We did an experiment. We watched to see what happened. We measured. We marked what we saw on our papers. We told what happened.)*

   Record student responses to steps 3 and 4 on a chart.

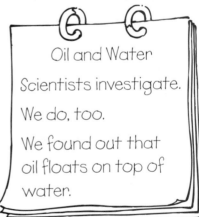

Oil and Water
Scientists investigate.
We do, too.
We found out that
oil floats on top of
water.

How Is Sound Made?

Materials

- paper cups
- rubber bands
- paper towel tubes
- record sheet on page 77, reproduced for each student
- minibook on pages 78–80, reproduced for each student

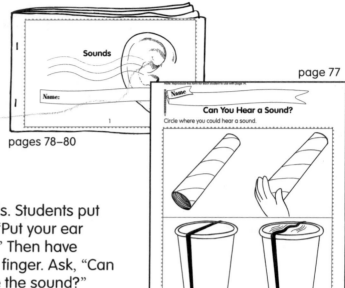

pages 78–80

page 77

Steps to Follow

1. Pass out paper cups and rubber bands. Students put a rubber band around their cup. Say, "Put your ear near the cup. Can you hear anything?" Then have students pluck the rubber band with a finger. Ask, "Can you hear something now? What made the sound?" *(The rubber band made the sound. The rubber band wiggled. That made the sound.)*

   Explain that sound is made when something "wiggles" (vibrates). When the rubber band was plucked it wiggled (vibrated). That is how the sound was made.

2. Collect the paper cups and rubber bands, and give each student a paper towel tube. Have them put their mouth up to one end of the tube and speak into it. Ask, "What did you hear? Could the sound travel through the tube?" Then have students completely cover one end of the tube with a hand. Have them speak into the tube again. Ask, "What did you hear?" (They may hear a muffled sound. If some students did hear a muffled sound, ask, "Was the sound as clear as before?") Ask, "What do you think stopped the sound? Could the sound travel through your hand?"

   Explain that their hands did stop the sound from moving through the air. We can hear a sound only if nothing stops it on the way to our ears.

3. Using page 77, students record the results of the investigation.

4. Ask students to recall how they acted like scientists. *(We did an experiment. We listened to see what happened. We marked what we heard on our papers. We told what happened.)*

   Record student responses to steps 2 and 4 on a chart.

5. Read and discuss the minibook on pages 78–80.

Logbook

Include these pages in each student's logbook.

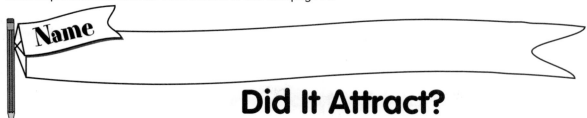

Name

Did It Attract?

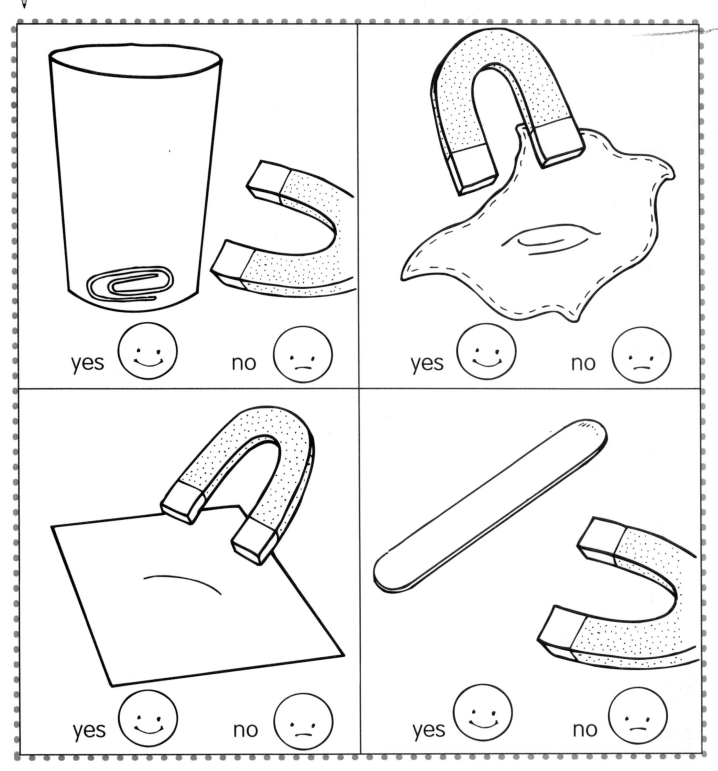

yes   no   yes   no

yes   no   yes   no

Name

What Happened to the Water and Oil?

Circle the picture.

Note: Reproduce this form for each student to use with page 74.

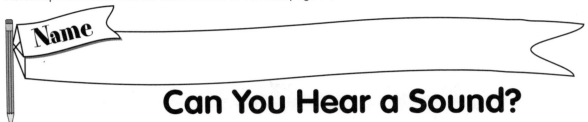

Can You Hear a Sound?

Circle where you could hear a sound.

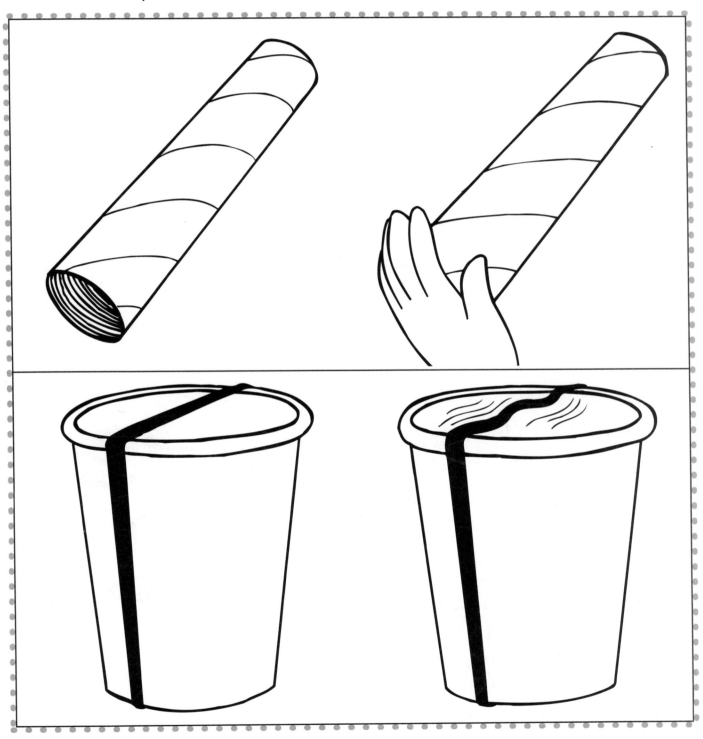

Learning to Be a Scientist • EMC 872

Learning to Be a Scientist • EMC 872

Sounds

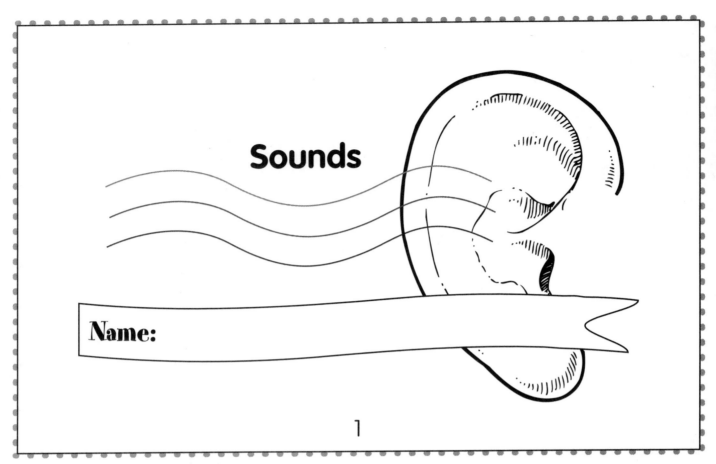

Name:

1

Sounds may be loud.

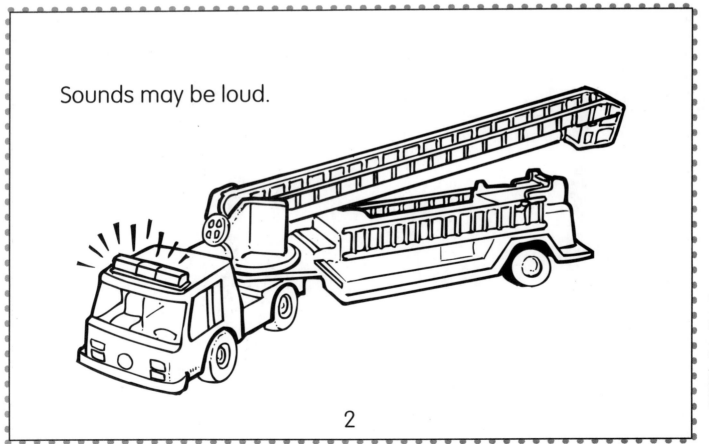

2

Sounds may be quiet.

3

Sounds may be noisy.

4

Sounds may be pleasant.

5

Learning to Be a Scientist • EMC 872

But all sounds happen when something vibrates.

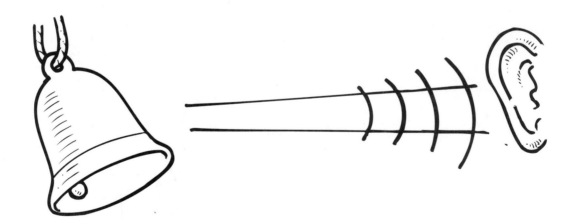

The sound moves through the air to your ear.
The sound moves through your ear to your brain.
Then you hear.

6